Strike/Slip

BOOKS BY DON McKAY

POETRY

Air Occupies Space 1973

Long Sault 1975

Lependu 1978

Lightning Ball Bait 1980

Birding, or desire 1983

Sanding Down This Rocking Chair on a Windy Night 1987

Night Field 1991

Apparatus 1997

Another Gravity 2000

Camber: Selected Poems 1983-2000 2004

Strike/Slip 2006

ESSAYS

Vis à vis: Fieldnotes on Poetry and Wilderness 2001

Deactivated West 100 2005

Strike/Slip

DON McKAY

McCLELLAND & STEWART

LIBRARY AND ARCHIVES CANADA CATALOGUING IN PUBLICATION

McKay, Don, 1942–
Strike/slip / Don McKay.

ISBN-13: 978-0-7710-5543-0
ISBN-10: 0-7710-5543-9

I. Title.

PS8575.K28S87 2006 C811′.54 C2005-906040-9

We acknowledge the financial support of the Government of Canada through the Book Publishing Industry Development Program and that of the Government of Ontario through the Ontario Media Development Corporation's Ontario Book Initiative. We further acknowledge the support of the Canada Council for the Arts and the Ontario Arts Council for our publishing program.

Text design by Sean Tai
Typeset in Aldus by M&S, Toronto
Printed and bound in Canada

This book is printed on acid-free paper that is 100% recycled, ancient-forest friendly (100% post-consumer recycled).

McClelland & Stewart Ltd.
75 Sherbourne Street
Toronto, Ontario
M5A 2P9
www.mcclelland.com

3 4 5 10 09 08 07

Contents

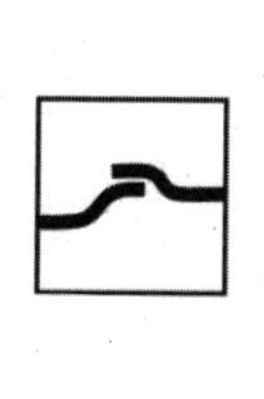

ASTONISHED –

astounded, astonied, astunned, stopped short
and turned toward stone, the moment
filling with its slow
stratified time. Standing there, your face
cratered by its gawk,
you might be the symbol signifying eon.
What are you, empty or pregnant? Somewhere
sediments accumulate on seabeds, seabeds
rear up into mountains, ammonites
fossilize into gems. Are you thinking
or being thought? Cities
as sand dunes, epics
as e-mail. Astonished
you are famous and anonymous, the border
washed out by so soft a thing as weather. Someone
inside you steps from the forest and across the beach
toward the nameless all-dissolving ocean.

PETRIFIED –

your heart's tongue seized
mid-syllable, caught by the lava flow
you fled. Fixed,
you stiffen in the arms of wonder's dark
undomesticated sister. Can't you name her
and escape? You are the statue
that has lost the entrance into art,
wild and incompetent,
you have no house. Who are you?
You are the crystal that picks up
its many deaths.
You are the momentary mind of rock.

LOSS CREEK

He went there to have it
exact. The broken prose of the bush roads.
The piles of half-burnt slash. Stumps
high on the valley wall like sconces
on a medieval ruin. To have it tangible.
To carry it as load rather than as mood
or mist. To heft it – earth measure,
rock measure – and feel its raw drag without phrase
for the voice or handle for the hand.
He went there to hear the rapids curl around
the big basaltic boulders saying
husserl husserl, saying I'll
do the crying for you, licking the schists
into flat skippable discs. That uninhabited laughter
sluicing the methodically shorn valley.
He went there to finger the strike/slip
fissure between rock and stone between Vivaldi's
waterfall and the wavering note a varied thrush
sets on a shelf of air. Recognizing the sweet
perils rushing in the creek crawling
through the rock.
He knew he should not trust such
pauseless syntax.
That he should just say no.
But he went there just the same.

PRECAMBRIAN SHIELD

Ancient and young, oldest
bone of the planet that was just
last week laid bare by the blunt
sculpting of the ice: it seemed a land designed
to summon mammals – haunched and shouldered,
socketed. Each lake we entered
was a lens, curious and cold
that brought us into focus.
Would I go back to that time,
that chaste and dangerous embrace?
Not unless I was allowed,
as carry-on, some sediment that has since
accumulated, something to impede the
passage of those days that ran through us
like celluloid. Excerpts from the book of loss.
Tendonitis. Second thoughts. Field guides.
Did we even notice
that the red pine sprang directly from the rock
and swayed in wind like gospel choirs?
Not us. We were muscle loving muscle, drank
straight from the rivers ran the rapids threw
our axes at the trees rode the back of every moose
we caught mid-crossing put our campfires out
by pissing on the flames. We could tell you
how those fuck-ups in *Deliverance*
fucked up: (1) stupid tin canoe (2) couldn't
do the J-stroke (3) wore life jackets (4) didn't
have the wit to be immortal

and ephemeral as we were. Sometimes,
in Tom Thomson's paintings you can see
vestigial human figures, brushstrokes
among brushstrokes. Would I go back
to that time, those lakes? Not without my oft-repeated dream
of diving for the body – possibly my own, possibly the lost
anonymous companion's – and surfacing to gulp in air
(the granite ridges watching, the clouds above them vacant
and declarative) and plunging once again into transparent
unintelligible depths.

SONG OF THE SAXIFRAGE TO THE ROCK

Who is so heavy with the past as you,
Monsieur Basalt? Not the planet's most muscular
depressive, not the twentieth century.
How many fingerholds
have failed, been blown or washed away, unworthy
of your dignified *avoirdupois*, your strict
hexagonal heart? I have arrived to show you, first
the interrogative mood, then secrets of the niche,
then Italian. Listen, slow one,
let me be your fool, let me sit
on your front porch in my underwear
and tell you risqué stories about death. Together
we will mix our dust and luck and turn ourself
into the archipelago of nooks.

ALLUVIUM

You wake, it wants you,
your room is *fleuve*. No use
hiding underneath the covers,
no use clinging to the lamp. It bears away
your diary, your mystery, your dresser
bobs off like a basket of reeds.
There goes the lamp you might have clung to,
trailing its muskrat tail,
there goes the laundry to its long last rinse.
The arms of your octopus, formerly
alarm clock, clutch, grabbing
like a teenage lover like a two-year-old it wants you
it won't wait for you to die
to lick the letters from your name.
Your old heart,
driven by its pell-mell bloodstream, spins,
legs on a runaway bike, you wake,
your room is *fleuve*, you're flotsam,
you're also-ran, you're all the riff-raff Noah
had no room for, uncountable
Canada geese and not-quite-standard moose,
you're everyone who ever
missed the playoffs, it wants you,
you have to go, already you can feel you're
somewhere else, deposited,
you're washed up in some other life as
insubstantial as a stone.

POND

Eventually water,
having been possessed by every verb –
been rush been drip been
geyser eddy fountain rapid drunk
evaporated frozen pissed
transpired – will fall
into itself and sit.
                                        Pond. Things touch
or splash down and it
takes them in – pollen, heron, leaves, larvae, greater
and lesser scaup – nothing declined,
nothing carried briskly off to form
alluvium somewhere else. Pond gazes
into sky religiously but also
gathers in its edge, reflecting cattails, alders,
reed beds and behind them, ranged
like taller children in the grade four photo,
conifers and birch. All of them inverted, carried
deeper into sepia, we might as well say
pondered. For pond is not pool,
whose clarity is edgeless and whose emptiness,
beloved by poets and the moon, permits us
to imagine life without the accident-
prone plumbing of its ecosystems. No,
the pause of pond is gravid and its wealth
a naturally occurring soup. It thickens up
with spawn and algae, while,
on its surface, stirred by every

whim of wind, it translates air as texture –
mottled, moiré, pleated, shirred or
seersuckered in that momentary ecstasy from which
impressionism, like a bridesmaid, steps. When it rains
it winks, then puckers up all over, then,
moving two more inches into metamorphosis,
shudders into pelt.

Suppose Narcissus
were to find a nice brown pond
to gaze in: would the course of self-love
run so smooth with that exquisite face
rendered in bruin undertone,
shaken, and floated in the murk
between the deep sky and the ooze?

DEVONIAN

Then someone says "four hundred million years" and the words
tap dance with their canes and boaters through
the spotlight right across the stage unspooling out the
stage door down the alley through the dark
depopulated avenues (for everyone is at the theatre) toward
the outskirts where our backyards bleed off into
motel
        rentall
                stripmall
                        U-haul past willowscruff, past ancient
rusting mercuries along the lovers' lanes the coyotes lure
our family pets down all those creekbanks where we
always did whatever anyway and left our bodies
blurring into brush the words slur into is it sand or
is it snow that blows its messages across
the highway through the headlight beam the dried-up
memories of water how the waves were how
the light that fell so softly through the depths was
intercepted by the lobe-finned fishes flickering among the
members of the audience still staring at the empty stage – four
hundred *million* years, yes, that's a long
long time ago.

QUARTZ CRYSTAL

It rests among the other stones on my desk – small chunks of granite, wafers of schist and slate – but it has clearly arrived from another dimension. While the others call, in the various dialects of gravity, to my fingers, the quartz crystal is poised to take off and return to its native aether. Some act of pure attention – Bach's D Minor concerto for instance – was hit by a sudden cold snap and fell, like hail, into the present. Here it lives in exile, a bit of locked Pythagorean air amid the pleasant clutter of my study: simple, naked, perilously perfect.

Just the same, I can pick it up, I can number its faces, I can hold its slim hexagonal columns in my fingers like empty pencils. Who do I think I am, with my little dish of stones, my ballpoint pen, my shelf of books full of notions, that I should own this specimen of earth's own artifice, this form before mind or math, its axes reaching back to the Proterozoic, its transparence the Zen before all Zen? It becomes clear that I must destroy my watch, that false professor of time, and free its tiny slave. No problem – a few taps with a piece of Leech River schist and the deed is done. But more is required. What? Off with my clothes; how else but naked should we approach the first of symmetries? Still insufficient, I can tell, although I can also feel waves of dismay radiating from my reference books, their mute embarrassment on my behalf. It is just the sort of thing they feared might happen when the first stones moved into the neighbourhood.

What next? Unfortunately, it appears I must set aside my fingers and thumbs, those tricky manipulators who have so busily converted rock to stone, who perpetrated the pyramids and silicon valley: go clasp yourselves in the dark until you learn to sit still and attend. More?

> I give up baseball, with its derivative threes
> and dreams of diamond.
> I forswear the elegant pairs and numbered runs
> of minuet and cribbage.
> I renounce the fugue. Dialectic,
> I bid you adieu. And you,
> my little poems, don't imagine I can't hear you
> plotting under your covers, hoping to avoid
> your imminent depublication.

While the crystal floats like a lotus on my palm, bending the light from a dying star to dance upon my coffee cup this fine bright Cenozoic morning.

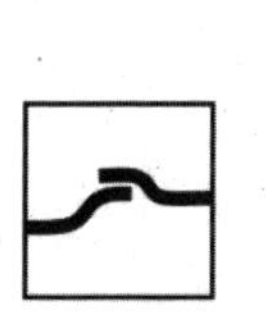

WAITING FOR SHAY

I

Summon it from sea mist: a dark shape
afloat on its barge in the half-air half-
water dreamtime of the coast. It may seem
a sort of monument, possibly a squashed Rodin
or the Vienna Philharmonic smelted down,
containerized and shipped on a drawn-out
tremulous Wagnerian chord, *frisson,*
foreboding, *liebestod,* up the strait
toward us. What is coming, we might ask, as the mist
lifts a flirtatious hem to give a glimpse
of massive body, petrified
rhinoceros or else some manic futurist's
reclining nude. On the shore
among the bristling Sitka spruce the mist is fingerless
caress, taking leave and entering, continuously
making threshold out of edge. And the forest, does it sense
the coming of another brand of predator
out there on the strait? Is this just
another beetle in a string of permutations
variously carapaced and horned, something
that might burrow, make place
for itself and propagate and lend its pattern
to the weave the way engraver beetles
leave a writing in the wood?
Does the forest simply go on making moss
and rot and whispering translations of translations, rain
into leaf into berry into bear as Shay
slides by on the tide?

II

Engine, ingenuity: how could we not love it?
Four-fifths animal, eats wood and water, breathes,
whistles, relieves itself of pressure with a sigh,
and harnesses the power of the sneeze to haul
its mass of gears and rods and
big avuncular belly up the ridge. Asthmatic,
cheerful, clockwork-clever,
tough as a troll, tough as a suit of armour that has long
outlived its knight, Shay is for sure
the brand-new neolithic monster for the job.

III

At the booming ground the wharf
extends its arm. The tracks reach
up the river valley as its spurs will also
reach up tributary creeks to make a stiff
tree-diagram that imitates the watershed
in iron. Waiting for Shay.
When the barge arrives the sleeping shape
will wake and start to breathe and
build a head of steam, accumulating wrath
like a hell-fire preacher. Then,
in a series of sharp
expostulations – work work work –
crank itself ashore. And then
the clock's wound up.

STUMPAGE

How the slash looks: not
ruin, abattoir, atrocity; not
harvest, regen, working
forest. How it looks. The way it
keeps on looking when we look away,
embarrassed. How it gawks,
with no nuance or subterfuge
or shadow. How it seems to see us now
as we see it. Not quick.
Not dead.

THE CANOE PEOPLE

Then they set off, they say.
After they had travelled a ways,
a wren sang to one side of them.
They could see that it punctured
a blue hole through the heart
of the one who had passed closest to it, they say.

– Ghandl, "Those Who Stay a Long Way Out to Sea,"
tr. Robert Bringhurst

They're out there, the unformed ones,
shapes in sea mist, half-
coagulated air, in their mossy
second-hand canoe. They're out there, the one
who holds the sky up, and the one who runs on
water, having no names to hang on,
old man's beard to branch, or fasten onto,
kelp to rock, or live in, hermit crab
to whelk shell. Out there,
sticking their soft canoe-nose into every cove
and inlet, the one who holds the bow pole and the
one who always bails, knowing nothing, having no raven side
and eagle side to think with, maundering their wayless way
among the islands, and now even
into English with its one-thing-then-
another-traffic-signalled syntax: out there, never
having heard their keel's bone-crunch on the beach, the terrible
birth cry of the plot, out there, the one who floats

the falcon feather, the one with bulging eyes, and the one
I almost recognize, already victim of the wren's bright
hammered music, bravely wearing in his heart that
delicate blue hole through which, I think,
he listens.

SONG FOR THE SONG OF THE CHIPPING SPARROW

Let's go. Let's gargle into song. Let's
clear our phlegm-clogged
fucked-up throats let's stutter our
dumb way into what
comes next. Take death rattle, take
automatic rifle fire, take t-t-t-t- Tommy Moss
day after day in grade two failing
to finish his name, let's
wrench them from their torments,
pass them through this skull-capped
bright-eyed sparrow in the spruce and into
morning's rah-rah for itself. Let's go.
For we shall be changed.

FIRST PHILOSOPHIES

The coastal trail: a line of thought for those
obsessed with origin, fugitives from history's
inland labyrinth. We hug the shore, hopeful,
amorous, smitten by the prospect of cosmogony
writ suddenly and large. One day,
watched by wind-carved clouds, it's clear
that everything derives from air, and perches,
not quite hovering. Another day it's fire:
the sea sweats and the basalt cliff
remembers magma. Just last week
the kinglets were so boastful in their
tinkerings I knew they'd been
first schemers of the logos, starting with staunch
Sitka spruce for shelter and for pinning down
their kingdom's western edge.
But today,
mist and drizzle up and down the coast,
a damp soul's best. Vague,
serendipitous among the pebbles, I've acquired and lost
a trove of wafers, faces, lozenges,
one great auk's egg, two milk teeth shed by sharks, and –
check this out – a red-black kidney stone once
passed by Apollo.
As I toss it, thoughtfully,
back to the surf, I realize that, yes,
everything derives from rock, rock that,
under these soft auspices,
suffers the insufferable ocean.

SONG FOR THE SONGS OF THE COMMON RAVEN

You could say it carries, you could say
dwells. *Corvus corax*: even in Latin
you can hear that smoke-and-whisky brogue –
croak, curruck, and (swallowing the syllable)
tok. You could say a fierce
unsayable secret has possessed the voice,
which has to speak and must not tell and so
is hollowed out and rendered terminally
hoarse. Of its brutal
seismic histories, its *duende,*
it says nothing. Nothing of the flowing and bending of rock,
of the burning going down and coming
up again as lava. Of rogue gods
loitering among the hemlocks nurturing the urge
to break out into body it conspicuously
does not sing. While sending messages that might
say "Watch your asses, creatures
of the Neogene" or might say "Baby,
bring it on."

SPECIFIC GRAVITIES: #76 (MARBLE)

To whom we turn to be
momentous, to be
monumental, to be
meant. As I browse
among the statues it appears
that marble is the way eternity
confers itself on breasts, it seems
that even pubic hair (David's,
for example), if redone in fine Carrara
marble, can become a simulacrum of the absolute,
one flare of graven
everliving fire.

But then,
on my way home, I take
a shortcut through the graveyard
and get mixed signals from the stones.
Are these the sculpted entrances to rooms
(*de lux*, I guess) located elsewhere?
Or should we think of them as exits –
holes the dead fell through
which we have squared up, plugged, and,
putting the best face upon it,
polished?

And this: once,
in Limerick, in a tiny tourist trap,
I came upon an egg of Connemara marble.
Heavy in the hand it was,
heavy as an egg whose embryo

foresaw its end, heavy as the one egg laid
by Schopenhauer's chicken. The past perfect
spoke to my fingers, who had fallen for it,
hard. "See that window?
Throw me through it. *Now.*"

"STRESS, SHEAR, AND STRAIN THEORIES OF FAILURE"

They have never heard of lift
and are – for no one, over and over – cleft. Riven,
recrystallized. Ruined again. The earth-engine
driving itself through death after death. Strike/slip,
thrust, and the fault called normal, which occurs
when two plates separate.
Do they hearken unto Orpheus, whose song
is said to make them move? Sure.
This sonnet hereby sings that San Fran-
cisco and L.A. shall, thanks to its chthonic shear,
lie cheek by jowl in thirty million
years. Count on it, mortals. Meanwhile,
may stress shear strain attend us. Let us fail
in all the styles established by our lithosphere.

UTTER

Utmost, remote. To be there
when pain finds words. That place
past place where history goes mute and myth
withers. Where the only signs
are the stray marks made by tools
on the margin of the task:
the utter left by the brute
weight of the piano. By the locomotive
grinding and polishing its tracks.
By my father's wheelchair
over and over scraping the frame
on the bathroom door. The utter
of our neolithic selves
knapping the rock, flaking
flint from chert, generation after
generation the dreadful craft by which
we etch a living. Work plus knack
plus luck. To slip that edge
between the ribs of grazing ungulates
the size of minivans. To reach
into the rock and drag forth
Inco. To be there when pain finds
words and tastes them acrid and metallic
on its raw tongue. Uttered.

As I approach the high sandstone cliff with its stacked, individual, terribly numerable varves, I think of George from group, who was unable either to stop collecting newspapers or to throw them out. He would describe – not without some pride, or at least amazement at his own extremity – how his basement, then living room, then bedroom had over the years become filled in with stacks of the *Globe and Mail*, the *Sun*, and the *Glengarry News*, all layered sequentially, until he was reduced to living in middle parts of his hallway and kitchen, his life all but occluded by sedimented public time. Unlike George's collection (which of course I saw only in my mind's eye), the cliff's is open to the eroding elements, so that bits have fallen off to form a talus slope of flat, waferlike platelets at its base. This one in my hand has been clearly imprinted by a leaf – simple, lanceolate, probably an ancestor of our ash or elder. Published but vestigial, gone like an anonymous oriental poet, its image still floating on the coarse grains of summer.

On the flip side, winter. Under the eyelid of the ice. How often I thought of writing you, but the pen hung over the page. All the details on the desk too shy to be inscribed. To settle, to hesitate exquisitely, at last to lie, zero among zeroes. Much listening then, but no audience. Rhetoric elsewhere. Language itself has long since backed out of the room on tiptoe.

Sometimes we believe that we must diagnose the perils of the winter varve, and so do our talk-show hosts and shrinks, who number its shades and phases as though it were pregnancy *renversé,* with suicide at the end instead of a baby. As though death were really death. As though the unspoken were failure. Having misread even the newspapers. Having been deaf to the music of the beech leaves, who will cling to their branches until spring, their copper fading to transparency, making a faint metallic clatter.

ABANDONED CABLE

Tangles of it by these overgrown
former bushroads, stiff constrictors
left to rust mid-writhe, the unfurled
unshriven entrails of the industrial
revolution. No point
preaching that all must rot, that everything
becomes ecology. This is the snarl
that strangled Laocoön, yarded
megatons of timber and erased
the forest that once was.
This is how the will
will manage its retirement: angry, kinked,
still waiting for its old buddy donkey-puncher to show up,
to step, pot-bellied and profane,
from the salmonberry bramble, build
a head of steam out of brag and booze
and show these soft-hearted
po-mo cappuccinos
something about work.

GNEISS

On the Isle of Lewis, be sure to stop at Callanish and spend some time at the circle of standing stones erected by our neolithic ancestors.

– Touring Scotland by Automobile

There is not much raw rock in that sentence, with its persuasive sibilants, not much scarp or grunt to remember the penalties paid – the load of it, the drag, the strained backs, smashed hands, and other proto-industrial injuries. It was not so long before this, not one whole afternoon as measured in the lifetimes of those upright slabs, that our ancestors had themselves achieved the perpendicular. Now they required that some of the rocks that comprised their island should stand up with them against the levelling wind and eroding rain. And further, that they should form lines leading to the most common and hopeful of human signs – the circle of connection, of return. They insisted that rock be stone.

From across the heath it appears – and perhaps this testifies to the brilliance of our ancestors as landscape artists – that the amiable rocks have taken this on themselves, getting up as you or I might do, as a sign of respect. By presenting themselves in a rough circle they are simply performing a courtesy, like ships flying the flag of a country they are passing through. They arrange themselves into an image of the eternity we crave rather than the brute infinity we fear.

But close up it is more likely to be the commotion of stress lines swirling within each slab that clutches at the heart – each stone a pent rage, an agon. None of the uniform grey of limestone, that prehistoric version of ready-mix concrete, in which each laid-down layer adds to the accumulated weight that homogenizes its predecessors. Think instead of Münch's *The Scream* with its contour lines of terror; then subtract the face. Or you could turn on the weather channel to observe those irresponsible isobars scrawling across the planet. Imagine our ancestors tracing these surfaces, whorled fingertip to gnarled rock, reading the earth-energy they had levered into the air. They had locked the fury into the fugue and the car crash into the high-school prom. They engineered this dangerous dance. Better stop here. Better spend some time.

APOSTROPHE

Protero, palaeo, meso, ceno:
I had, I thought,
a thing to say as I approached
the columns of angular basalt. But all those
rough chateaux were shut, their epochs
slammed, their hours immured.
The spells of textbooks
echoed, so much gabbling Greek.
I thought of earth,
how it remembers us and calls our
nutrient-rich bodies and nostalgia-heavy heads
home to its humus.
Not basalt.
Rude, out of reach, it listens
inward to some proto-music played
in zero-zero time, the songs
of continents colliding or the slow
churn of current through its mother magma.
I had a thing to say about
our common residence in time, or was that
(here I planned to raise a fine
ironic eyebrow) mutual incarceration?
Instead I stood there,
snubbed, mostly water, growing younger
at a rate my poor life can't allow.

*

What basalt sheds, moon
seems to solicit: handless clock, we say,
stopped heart, pockmarked mirror, as though one
perfect metaphor might cure
its clinical depression.
False advertising, as we half suspect,
designed to keep us babbling while the moon
hunkers on its dark side, deaf, blind rock
staring into cold infinity. But even this suspicion
fails to stem the tide – sonatas, pop songs, manic
dances, orgies, docudramas, and of course the poets
scribbling our skeptical hearts out, o
insoluble aspirin, o insomnia's forty-watt bulb, uncaring
vanity press impresario, we say,
better you, with your pretended
and inconstant interest,
than nothing.

FULL MOON, CAMPBELL RIVER

It calls infinity from the grass
and frosts each blade.
Burnishes the current. Separates trees
into ghost-self and shadow-self. In its grip
loneliness sheds its longing for a friend
to walk by the water, to listen in its
own tongue, uninhabited,
immaculate. All body
belongs to the river, black-silver,
micro-muscled, a rush of inchoate creatures urging
in and out of incarnation, otter-back,
seal-back, flank, snakeskin, someone's left arm
arcing by the far shore overseen by squat
swart psychopompic gulls –

                                        me interrupting, whoa,
whoa, let's go inside and get warm,
let's listen to *Ideas* on the CBC –

                                                    while loneliness
goes on intoning river, river,
unsayer of sameness, undersong,
anti-information, river in whom no one –
          not the myth-teller, not the holy fool,
          not the mad entranced
          fly fisherman –
steps twice, only the dubious gods and the divine
spectacularly mortal salmon.

PHILOSOPHER'S STONE

— and when, after I've wasted a lifetime looking,
picking over eskers, browsing beaches, rock shops, slag,
when, after I've up and quit, you suddenly
adopt me, winking from the gravel of the roadside
or the rip-rap of the trail or the
jewels of the rich;
when you renounce your wilderness and move in,
living in my pocket as its sage, as my third,
uncanny testicle, the wise one,
the one who will teach me to desire
only whatever happens;
when you happen in my hand as nothing
supercooled to glass, as the grey
watersmooth rock that slew Goliath or the stone
no one could cast; when you come
inscribed by glaciers, lichened, mossed,
packed with former lives inside you like a dense
mass grave;

when you cleave,

when you fold,
when you gather sense as *omphalos, inukshut,*
cromlech, when you rift in the stress
of intolerable time;
when you find me as the moon
found Li Po in his drunken boat,
when you speak to my heart of its heaviness, of the soft

facts of erosion, when you whisper in that
tongueless tongue it turns out,
though it can't be,
we both know —

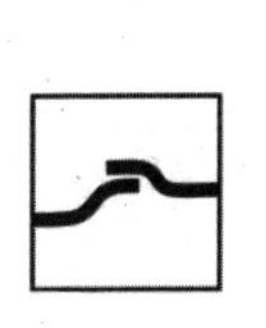

HORSE PULL

It is important that the load be ugly and anonymous, neither rock nor stone but concrete slabs – abstract utility unfallen into this use or that. This is part of its gift to us, as we sit in the bleachers with our backs and shoulders clenching, hauling along with Mac and Red – that it might as well be the nine-to-five, the chemo, the kid you haven't heard from since way before Christmas. That it might be the whole mess. It is important that they have names like Mac and Red, Jack and Bill, Dick and Pete, sometimes stretching another syllable to Benny and Rusty, never to the drawing-room decadence of thoroughbreds. No Ambrosial Dancer, no Colonel's Fancy, no Moon Walker. No Hercules. Mac and Red haul 3000, 4000, 5000, finally up to 10,000 pounds through the dust, huge-haunched, their big hearts beating in unison, taking the whole heave of it through their chests. It is important that it is mammal and before the wheel, and that it nevertheless drags the nineteenth century, pound by pound, into the twenty-first. They are the best of brawn, before it goes on the rampage or sulks in its tent. The heart is like everything, as The Heart Sutra and country and western reveal; but what it is, is muscle.

Here comes Dick and Pete, with Yves behind them holding the reins, circling around the sled with its stack of slabs, a failed ziggurat called 9500 pounds. The assistant picks up the hitch with its hook and Yves has them sidle and back up to the sled, a little whoa, a little shuffle, a little haw Dick, then the hook drops into the eye. At this point some teams will jerk the load, slamming into the inertia to break its surface quickly. But Yves has Dick and Pete settle, settle, they know this gathering, this centring of themselves, whoa Dick, whoa Pete, their hooves pressing into the ground, a kind of massage, building rhythm like dancers creating circles in their bodies, currents passed haunch to haunch until they're moving in synch like a massive immobile rhumba. Then – one flick of the reins – they pour all that energy into drag: thirteen feet six inches.

And it is important that the big John Deere should watch from the sidelines, *deus ex machina,* with its eloquent large-treaded wheels and high glass cab; that it should have been loaned by the farm implement dealer; and that it should, once Dick and Pete have been unhooked from the load, haul it effortlessly back to the starting line for Jack and Bill.

KEN

Loaded, you lug the forest
stick by stick to its
demise. Empty, but still revved, still
unsatisfied, you hump yourself, rear end
buggering the fore like two *Tyrannosaurus*
rexes stuck mid-thrust, the pincer
from the front end reaching back
to clench the nether's tail, clocking
130 klicks in the passing lane. Situation
normal. "Kenworth," you declare,
grinning through your smart chrome Richard Nixon
grille.

In all the best hells
suffering occurs in public. But you, o Ken,
I would sentence to the private life
you loathe, parked in a cave, alone,
assailed by doubts dressed up
as bats, your eons
measured out in drips. Grief,
which you call rust,
becomes you as you crane to hear
the song of mother rock.

The song to which you are –
like us, your heartsick, horror-
stricken Doctor Frankensteins –
quite deaf.

APRÈS CHAINSAW

Everything listening at me:
the stumps oozing resin, the birdsong
bouncing off my head like sonar,
the bludgeoned air with its fading
after-echoes. I think of people
herded to a square, staring
at the man on the platform.
Whatever I say now
will be strictly interpreted
and parsed. Is this the way it works,
locking you, stunned, in the imperative,
making a weapon of each tool?
Why can't we just bury innocence instead of
wrecking it over and over, as if
it could never die
enough?
What I want to say is
somewhere a man steps
softly into a hemlock-and-fir-fringed
pause. Heart full.
Head empty. His lost path
scrawls away behind him. A blue
dragonfly with double wings zags, hovers,
zags. A flicker he can't see
yucks its ghost laugh
into the thin slant light.

HIKING WITH MY SHADOW

Though it has to bushwhack
while I take the trail, it keeps pace
perfectly, folding over boulders,
skimming the stumps and alder scrub, bulging
then flattening, sometimes as a puddle,
sometimes as a hunchback or a baby grand,
always as nothing, nothing
that loves me and that dogs my tracks
better than a dog.
                                        Patient companion, little
ink lake, when I pause
you heel, and wait like a suitcase
while I squander my attention on a wren.
Just barely do I feel that faint
tug on my foot like someone
fumbling for a valve.
As though you knew that one day
I'll be yours, and flow
into that deflated body bag to be
its third dimension.
And our real life will begin.

SOLO

Dusk climbs the trunks and
spreads along the branches, then
summons its birds in rough
asymmetrical gestalts, wings
wincing the air, shifting like fine
polyphony, they waver and yaw, they
ride the wind that drives them,
and leave the heart in its little lit room.

VESPERS

In the abbey wood as the vesper bell begins to toll, waiting for a red-breasted nuthatch to decide whether it wants to come to my hand for a peanut or fly off. Bold empty headlines from the mineral world, each note trembling with echo, trying to stir itself into the air like its iron supplement. The nuthatch still uncertain, still perched on the Jack pine waving its needle-beak in my direction as though reading the situation with a wand.

I'm not so certain myself, suspended between the nasal air-within-air voice of the nuthatch and the great floated world-weight of the bell with its stony musical groans. All those forces that shaped the original rock – pressure, stress, heat – were actually slumbering ogres who've been tamed, and trained to sing. I think it is a simple song about time; or it may be that time is the singer. Something about translating its infinity into eternity so we can hear it without bleeding from the ears. Something about night falling.

With my arm held out this way, I might be asking the trees for alms; I might be hitchhiking. As so often, I have entered the condition of waiting and forgotten to watch, so the arrival of the nuthatch is a familiar lurch of the heart. A tiny black fire for an eye; a smudged red chest; feet on my finger like intelligent twigs. It takes the peanut with a sideways scoop and flies back to the pine it came from.

The bell's last gongs disintegrate. Their flakes fall to earth and begin to burrow back into it. Head down, the nuthatch is hiding its peanut under a flap of bark.

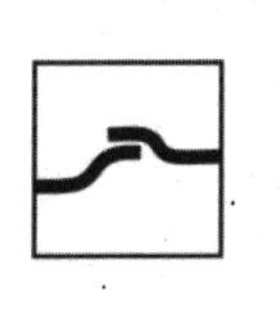

AS IF SPIRIT, AS IF SOUL

(i)

Lifting off, letting go, seizing leave as though
departure were the first act ever, stepping
into air as sigh, as outbreath, hum,
commotion, whirr,
it's out of here, it's shucked us like
high school, like some stiff
chrysalis it lets fall from invisible
unfolding wings.
And already we are saying
let there be, let there be
liftoff, let there be loss, let there be those
silver knives that swim in blood like sharpened
minnows, let there be those
tossed-off warbler phrases that dissolve in air before
the voice can manage to corral them, that exquisite thirst
whose satisfaction is another
larger thirst equipped with claws like question marks requiring
answers in the form of still another thirst and
though we recognize this evil as our own we also
recognize the camber of its nothing as it
lifts, as it glances,
as it vanishes.

(ii)

Still, something settles,
something stays. Something sedimentary
accumulates. Something
hearkens to the blues until it turns
inward to its own past tense. It sits
in the kitchen listening to us weep and gradually
fills up with plot and character like nineteenth-
century fiction. Finally, we might suppose,
it will evolve much as the emu
into flightlessness, with wings that hold the heat,
forgoing all those otherwheres to dwell among us
as a landed immigrant.

(iii)

Or is it

more like this: I don't know
how the house wren managed to get in,
but it was hard to get it out. It battered
at the window as though trying to call this stiff air
back to life, its panic
fanned by my efforts to help. Uppermost –
the wish that it would find the open door.
Deepest was the hope it never would – but
what that hope imagines coming next
is difficult to say. Probably a time out: house wren
perched on the fridge to cock its slender tail, me asking
would it care for some granola as it
empties another waterfall of notes
into the indrawn air of the kitchen.

DIPPER AT PARKINSON CREEK

Presto-critter, you are the creek's own
bright idea and your quicknesses – dart,
tilt, look, zip-across-the-rapids,
perch – inflect its flow. Each dip
curtseys to the mists, the crashes,
the rushed-over rocks, to the falls'
translucent lip with all ferocity
still soft inside it, dip
tilt
        dip. And then, like someone
casually committing suicide, you hop
right into the rapids.
What next, I wonder,
as an alder leaf drifts
down to the surface.
A far raven.
The creek's continuous
music of wash and loss.
"I venture to inquire . . ." when,
just as suddenly you hatch on a rock
mid-current, having lunched upon the bugs
and micro-bugs of trouble, one more
dip and you're off,
upstream, leaving a burbling song among the choruses
that eat their way into the laminated grey-green
schist of the Pacific Rim Terrane.

SONG FOR THE SONGS OF THE FALLEN LEAVES

So many vexing anonymities – shrugs,
aliases, crepitations, secrets of the séance,
secrets of the sea. Who goes there,
publishing its deep-fried alphabet? Who needs
fifty letters to say *sh*, twenty-five
articulating *f*? Maybe it's a flock of juncos
scritching the forest floor, or chipmunks,
or a bit of breeze
leafing through the pages of the *Tao Te Ching*.
Maybe it's the dead
come to visit with their dreadful lisps
and talk-show gossip from the other side,
or the subtext, a.k.a. the black bear who will
enter in Act III to marry us
or eat us up. Or maybe just those
mindless feet of yours, still
doing the goose-step, soft shoe,
goose-step through the washed-up
desiccated turf.

ASCENT WITH THRUSHES

1\.
Listen, I tell my knees,
as we pause at the twenty-somethinged
switchback: at each step
we are accompanied by air. Listen:
the phrase slides, heartlessly,
past pain, wonder, grief, into its
interrogative lift, no questions asked,
no special pause called art. It falls
carelessly uphill, I say, listen,
we should be so lucky.

2\.
Higher up, we pause to pant
while single buzzy
indigo-blue notes are drilled
toward us from the other side.
Spy-holes, probably,
so the sky can watch us
as we clamber toward it. As though
we were end-wise to the music.
As though we were
looking down the barrel of a song.

3\.
Among subalpine fir beside
the partly frozen lake some unseen
singer is – against the best advice

a poet ever gave –
praising the unsayable to the angel.
I listen in immaculate calm. It's only Churl
and Mort, those unruly
ears of mine, who slaver after every
empty phrase.

4.
Later in the parking lot
I stretch and thank my knees,
without whose efforts, et cetera,
et cetera. On the far side of the notice board
the day's selections (Swainson's,
Varied, Hermit) are being recapped and discussed,
exhaustively, in demotic
American Robin.

PINE SISKINS

Unseen in the pines the pine siskins
are unlocking the seeds from the pine cones, click
click click, as *chez soi* as Danes
eating danishes in Denmark. The chaff,
flung off, freckles the air,
the lawns, the parked cars,
and the notebook in my lap. Fallout,
I scrawl. Dross. Dun-coloured memos from entropy
recalling the blank page to its native
winter.

But who cares? Up there
the siskins party on, now and then
erupting into siskin song – upswept
ardent buzzes, part
wolf whistle, part raspberry, part Charles Ives'
"Unanswered Question":
tragic-comic operas crammed
into their opening arpeggia.

DEEP MIDWINTER

Snow had fallen, snow on snow
snow on snow
– Christina Rossetti

Once upon a time the sky's
eternal silence broke up into bits, fresh
new-angled nothings
sowing the wind with pique.
Not wing,
though it flies, nor spirit,
though it isn't and it is, nor song,
though it could be said to sing
inaudibly, and though it falls
it's liable to forget and float
or sift, indulged by gravity, as though
that hard-and-fast rule had gone
soft and slow.
Finally
it settles on the earth, eternal
silence once again, but
tangible, depthed, an unbreathed
breath.
Long ago –
it is always long ago –
before there were beds,
or blankets, or animals to wish
they had them, snow:
snow on snow
on snow.

IN AORNIS

Where each tangle in the foliage
is not a nest, where the wind
is ridden by machines. Aornis,
birdless land, whose uninflected sky extends
like rhetoric to the horizon, *idée*
fixe, tight as Tupperware. Each item
insular, insomniac, attended
by echo and clock. The letters
would rather be numbers, the numbers
disavow Pythagoras. Aornis,
where you don't need mysticism
and you don't need music
to do math. The unsung sun,
it turns out, comes up anyway,
while the rocks and lintels, UV bleached
and birdshit-free, are host
to no Xanthoria. In Aornis,
when it snows, the snow
weighs on the branches and the branches
bend beneath the weight. They know
no junco will descend to instigate
the tiny blizzard like a sneeze
which frees them. Only now and then
one will shrug and shed its load
like an old man who recalls an antique joke
and silently silvers the air.

feathers but no wings.
Time passes. The feathers
fade in the light, which regards them
softly and undoes
their delicate Velcro.

Look at me,
bones but no body.
Time passes. The bones
fall in love with the wind,
which teaches them to whistle.

Look, nails
but no fingers.
Time passes. The nails
erode in the rain
which is falling,
falling made visible,

made river.

Look at me.

SOME LAST REQUESTS

Of stone:

That oblivion be tempered
with remembrance and the limestone step be worn,

be softened by our ins and outs.
That swart chunks of granite

hold our tent down tight
when the wind blows all our tools away. That,

after I'm over,
you carry my name a little further on

till it gets past missing me. And if,
being fearful,

it still declines to fade, feed it,
phoneme by phoneme,

to the hawk scream it so badly mimicked
with its last long I.

Or winter.

Of rock:
That you teach me, as they say,
(insincerely) in the love songs,

to forget.
That my words should kiss

their complex personalities goodbye and sink
into Loss Creek, into

Ink Lake, into Black
Duck Brook, seeking the coarse

democracy of till.
That you instruct my bones in the art

of living rough and allow my thoughts
to fray into the weathers they have long

loved from afar.
As to my pain, that fine

pre-echo of the infinite:
keep it.

Keep it safe.

Notes

Strike/slip: A strike/slip fault (in contrast to a thrust fault or a normal fault) is a high-angle fault along which rocks on one side move horizontally in relation to rocks on the other side with a shearing motion. Examples are the famous San Andreas Fault in western North America, the Great Glen Fault in Scotland, and the Loss Creek–Leech River Fault on southern Vancouver Island.

"Loss Creek": "I'll do the crying for you" is borrowed from Colleen Thibaudeau's poem "There's a waterfall in Iceland."

"Waiting for Shay": For the first half of the twentieth century, logging railroads were the most common means of hauling timber out of the forest to booming grounds on the coast. By 1924, there were seventy-four logging railroads operating on Vancouver Island, and at least two-thirds of them used the powerful, dependable Shay locomotive.

"Stumpage": "Regen" is forestry-speak for bush that is regenerating after being clear-cut.

"The Canoe People": Among the Haida, the canoe people are spirit beings who travel perpetually among the islands, appearing ashore only whenever a shaman opens a way. Before this first occurred, they did not realize that they were spirits or know who they were. See Ghandl of the Qayahl Llaanas, *Nine Visits to the Mythworld*, translated by Robert Bringhurst, Vancouver: Douglas and McIntyre, 2000.

"Stress, Shear, and Strain Theories of Failure": The title comes from Charles M. Nevin, *Principles of Structural Geology*, New York: John Wiley, 1949. Lines 9–12 refer to the fact that, since Los Angeles and San Francisco are both situated on the San Andreas Fault, they will lie alongside one another in about thirty million years at the present rate of movement.

"Utter": Used as a noun, *utter* means the irregular marks left on a surface by the vibration or too great pressure of a tool.

"Varves": These are alternating layers of coarse and fine sediment that have accumulated in an ancient lake and subsequently hardened into rock. The coarse layers accumulated during the summer months when streams carried silt and sand into the lake; the fine layers formed each winter when the surface was covered with ice, so that only slim grains of clay could settle to the bottom. See Steven M. Stanley, *Earth System History*, New York: Freeman, 1999.

"Full Moon, Campbell River": This poem was commissioned for Words on the Water, the Campbell River literary festival.

"In Aornis": The title is Greek and means "land without birds." Xanthoria is a common orange lichen that often derives the nitrogen it needs for growth from bird excrement.

Acknowledgements

Some of these poems have appeared in *Grain, Prairie Fire, The Fiddlehead,* and *Rampike;* some have appeared in chapbook form as *Varves,* from Extra Virgin in Edmonton.

"The Canoe People" appeared previously in *Vis à Vis* (Gaspereau, 2001). "Waiting for Shay," "Après Chainsaw," and "Philosopher's Stone" appeared, in different forms, in *Deactivated West 100* (Gaspereau, 2005).

Thanks to Tim, Stan, Roo, Kim, Dennis, Robert, and – as always – Jan, for long-term listening. I owe a special debt of gratitude to Barry Dempster, who edited the manuscript with exceptional care and finesse.

"Pond" is for Trevor Goward; "Full Moon, Campbell River" is for Trevor and Ruth McMonagle.

Some of these poems were composed during a residency at the Haig-Brown House in Campbell River. My thanks to the Haig-Brown Institute and the Canada Council for their support.

This book is dedicated to the memory of my parents, John and Margaret McKay.